Mindful thoughts for
# CITY DWELLERS

First published in the UK in 2018 by

*Leaping Hare Press*

An imprint of The Quarto Group
The Old Brewery, 6 Blundell Street
London N7 9BH, United Kingdom
**T** (0)20 7700 6700 **F** (0)20 7700 8066
www.QuartoKnows.com

British Library Cataloguing-in-Publication Data
A catalogue record for this book is available from the British Library

ISBN: 978-1-78240-568-9

This book was conceived, designed and produced by

*Leaping Hare Press*

58 West Street, Brighton BN1 2RA, UK

Publisher: *Susan Kelly*
Creative Director: *Michael Whitehead*
Editorial Director: *Tom Kitch*
Art Director: *James Lawrence*
Commissioning Editor: *Monica Perdoni*
Project Editor: *Jenny Campbell*
Editor: *Jenni Davis*
Illustrator: *Lehel Kovacs*

Printed in China

1 3 5 7 9 10 8 6 4 2

# Mindful thoughts for
# CITY DWELLERS

*The joy of urban living*

**Lucy Anna Scott**

*Leaping Hare Press*

# Contents

# INTRODUCTION
# Message from a
# City Lover

When I moved to London in my early twenties, I was like one of those characters from the films, like Buddy in *Elf* or Mick in *Crocodile Dundee,* who find themselves in the metropolis for the first time and totally bemused by it.

Raised in a tiny village under a vast sky, I was unprepared for urban life – a rookie who would flinch as an underground train came rattling and clattering into the station and hesitate as the doors hissed open, fearful of being trapped in their jaws. It was not unusual for me to leap on a train heading in the opposite direction to the way I wanted to go either, one that would eventually spit me out on to some outpost of mysterious and deserted-looking industrial units.

Fifteen years on, however, I'm a Londoner and committed urbanite. Those years taught me that living in the metropolis doesn't mean you cannot carve out a spiritually enriching life for yourself. To me, a happy, mindful existence comes from using your senses to engage with the environment, growing plants, marking the seasons, noticing the moon, being possession-light, living consciously. This is the nature of my days.

This mindful life has come from getting to know the city deeply, exploring its layers, burrowing beneath the noise, smog and crowds. I had come to the city to make a career but I never imagined that my life in it would teach me anything about a slower pace. Urban living, it is assumed, is too boisterous to provide peace, too pressured to allow time to connect – to the moment, to others and to ourselves.

It is my hope that this book will show you how nourishing a metropolis can be – an environment with the potential to help us to see more, hear more, feel more. While many urbanites idealize that time when we can trade in our postage-stamp-sized apartments for a quiet house by the sea, a natural landscape – as crucial as it is for the soul – cannot make us connect the way that being with humans can. I know, because I tried it.

When my other half and I had our first child, we began to wonder whether the city, much as we loved it, would be right for the long haul. I used to liken the city to a brilliant but unsuitable boyfriend: charming, fun, thrilling, but not marriage material. As we entered this fresh phase of our lives, we decided to decamp to a roomy house by the coast. We were living the dream, you might say. But I felt completely lost. I missed being part of a special kind of humanity. Enriching, inventive, ever-evolving and endlessly social, the urban community creates an inspiring energy that had kept me facing outward rather than inward. It had kept me connected to the world.

Back in the city, I now know what a powerful force for well-being togetherness is. That urban life is where I belong. And if the city can make a country girl feel this way, it can have that effect on anyone.

# Part of the
# Mindful City

A magazine once invited me to write an article on why I chose the city life when I had such a love for the natural landscape. I didn't know at the time that a rural existence didn't suit me, but I still had this instinct that the two aspects of my character weren't so paradoxical.

I've never felt I had to curtail my interest, or need, for the wild. In fact, it is life in the city that has shown me how fascinating it is when the natural world and the man-made world live cheek by jowl. Seeing a conservation garden thrive under a thundering flyover, or raptor's nest in the niche of a skyscraper, has revealed to me that the wild is much closer to the metropolis than we think.

What is more, that duality we have set up for ourselves –
that true nature belongs to the countryside, that it is
something we only need to protect in designated areas –
is a distinction that is becoming obsolete.

The successful city of tomorrow will be one that
embraces tree coverage as a way to keep us cool and the
air clean, one that supports the ecosystems that allow
us to grow food on urban farms and maintain pest-free
green spaces. It will be the city that sees a public park
as a priceless green lung and one that enables its
inhabitants to know the texture and rhythm of the
natural world.

Now that over half the world's population is urban
dwelling, it is cities that will be at the forefront of
reducing our impact upon the Earth. Only a mindful
city will be able to come together to innovate ways to
tackle climate change, create and facilitate green transport
and carbon-neutral buildings, and build infrastructure
that supports the generation of clean energy. Only
a mindful city will thrive in the future.

# A MEETING OF WORLDS

Many cities possess numerous raw materials to create healthier, happier places. Cities can be home to rare species you may never find anywhere else; in the city I live in, that includes bats, butterflies, spiders and plants. And I can rise with the sun to listen to the dawn chorus, and find streams so clean their waters sparkle.

But here, in the city, I am more able to live a sustainable life than I did when I lived rurally; urban density means I don't need a car to get everywhere – or indeed anywhere – and recycling is not a niche hobby. Ecologists have found that the concentration of populations and use of mass transit decreases human encroachment on natural habitats, while the apartments we live in are more energy-efficient than detached suburban houses. This means we have as equal an opportunity as anybody to find solutions that secure a sustainable planet, and a future for our species.

The metropolis encapsulates the tension between the human-made and the natural world in one physical place.

It is a battle that has been, and still is, too often won by *Homo sapiens*. And now it is dawning on us just how much this will hurt. But if we can find a better way of resolving these challenges in cities, where the pressures of accommodating and supporting huge populations are most acute, there is hope we can manage to coexist in a supportive, rather than antagonistic, fashion.

## ADOPT A TREE

Applying a touch of humanity to one square metre of the city can be a powerful action that is both fulfilling and beneficial for your neighbourhood. Adopting a street tree is one example. Take a newly planted sapling that's recently appeared near your home or workplace. Water it occasionally, loosen the straps that tether it to its stakes as it gains strength as a service to horticulture – but also to ensure the enduring well-being of your metropolis.

As the sapling's trunk matures from a skinny whip to a burly adult that can hold its own in a harsh, competitive environment, imagine the many city dwellers who will be able to take respite under the shade of its lush awning on a sweltering day, and enjoy the chance to inhale the pocket of fresh air the plant has gifted.

The idea that we might uncover mindfulness in the rubble of a city's problems may feel counter-intuitive. It might also seem a burden when day-to-day responsibilities are numerous, when many cities are so set in their old-school polluting ways – and are, today at least, doing just fine by them. But the joy of mindful action is in the optimism of it. Even in simple, small-scale ways we are able to feel hopeful that the city is not simply a crushing human jungle. The city can be – *is* – a place where humanity flourishes.

# Breathe with
# **the Trees**

It is years spent living in a city that has taught me
to appreciate the tree. In the rural landscape of my
childhood they were ten a penny, more trees than people
it seemed. This is not to say I didn't love them then –
they watched me through the years as I grew from the
child playing chase around their trunks to a teen sitting
under them on balmy nights, gossiping and drinking.

Arriving on the city's doorstep in my early twenties,
feeling deprived of clean air and the space I had always
known, it was the trees that I sought out most. Not
only the stately residents of the parks, but also those
that lined the streets. Even when I came upon one
rebelling against the hard rigour of a garden fence,

I would make sure to linger long enough to catch its scent, guess its age, gaze up at the patterns its canopy of leaves made against the sky.

Even now, as rooted to the city as I am, I still love to lean against an elderly species when I come across one. Like a nurturing grandparent, old trees always feel warm, mysteriously comfortable despite the roughness of their bark. To stand close to one and remember the generations they have observed come and go, and will do still, is a little lesson in perspective for those bad days, and on how brief our lives are in the great scheme, even compared with other earthly beings.

## DEEP BREATHS

Over the years, I've developed affection for certain specimens in the city, returning to the same trees time and again: a willow on the riverbank, its branches tangled in weed; a prolific mulberry in a park south-east of the city, whose fruit is the sweetest reward for the effort of the trek; a tulip tree in my local botanic garden that captures the breeze under its large maple-like leaves and plays with it in a captivating choreography.

Somehow, trees make me inhale more deeply than I do anywhere else. It is as if my body instinctively responds to the oxygen shrouded about them. I know that as I go about my business in the metropolis I subconsciously resist taking air in so fully, wary of the pollution. But when I see trees, those grand masters of air purification, I feel safer letting my lungs expand to their max.

Breathing deeply like this is a pick-me-up that feels as refreshing as a dip in the ocean. But it is crucial to remember that breathing well is so intrinsic to our state of mind that it's important to find times – and places – where we can regularly enjoy the restorative act of inhaling and exhaling. The shallow, high chest breathing we adopt while running between meetings, hunched over a desk or waiting for that delayed train keeps our hearts ticking. But it doesn't feed our bodies, or our minds for that matter, with the full health benefits of a deep, relaxed abdominal inhalation.

## THE RESTORATIVE MINUTE

We could label this practice 'the restorative minute'. This notion is the opposite of the New York minute, a phrase that expresses the intense compression of time in the Big Apple. Any urbanite can relate to this New York perspective on how the minutes and hours whip by, and how our physiology mirrors its fraught vibe.

The restorative minute, therefore, gives us permission to stop, recalibrate the breath and clear the mind. In this minute, you get to step aside – whether in thought, or physically interrupting whatever task you're doing – and observe your actions, noting how fully you are breathing, whether your body feels tight as it clings to stress.

This minute can be taken in your home, on a park bench in your lunch hour, even on the deserted floor of a gallery. Of course, the fresher the air, the better – so parks or churchyards, where there's usually plenty of vegetation, are the ideal spaces. Wherever you do it, the effect is the same: when the sixty seconds are up, mind and body feel calmed. Working from home allows me to steal a break easily, but even when I worked in a hectic open-plan office and on various shop floors, I found time to do what I considered then to be a quietly rebellious act.

Once you've reached your chosen oasis, begin by readjusting your posture so your shoulders are relaxed, sitting up or standing straighter to stretch out the spine and unclench the jaw. Take deep breaths in and out – inhale slowly through the nostrils, allowing the lungs to expand enough to feel your ribcage rise gently, and then slowly release the air in a steady stream, again through the nostrils, feeling the ribs fall back into place.

This practice allows us to be more sensitive to our anxiety levels when agitating through crowds. Apply breath control as you walk, breathing in for four to six paces and out for the same number.

After your minute is up, you may feel more alert and less quick to huff at anyone 'dithering' across your path. You may have noticed that during the exercise, you were thinking only about the nurturing sensation that comes when you inhale air right to the bottom of your lungs.

# A New
# Horizon

I once met a man who saw skyscrapers as mountains. He liked to hike them, from stairwell to rooftop, one building after the other, covering distances as vast as an expedition to Everest's peak. Adventure, for this explorer, meant having inquisitiveness about your surroundings; it is found and felt when you strive to look up, down and all around.

I never did ask him if he came across a group of birding enthusiasts, a merry band of men and women who rise with the dawn to congregate on the rooftop of one of London's tallest buildings. They head to the summit of this particular high-rise to watch for passing raptors and other wildlife.

23

All year round, the tower rewards these pilgrims with hallowed avian sightings – peregrines, sparrowhawks, buzzards, cormorants and herring gulls, moving among the bridges and art galleries and museums with the same lyricism as in their natural habitats.

From the rooftop, their human onlookers can perceive the metropolis as a landscape in three dimensions. We city dwellers spend so much time getting somewhere, eyes cast down, that pavements become our main topographical reference, and our only horizons are the stepped skylines – the nature of what lies beyond them we rarely stretch ourselves to imagine.

## DISCOVERING WILDNESS

Wild things impose no such boundaries on their vision. To a bird, an office building is another clifftop, a nesting site, a vantage point for hunting; to a free spirit with a backpack, glass, steel and concrete has every potential to excite and fulfil a primitive-born tendency to wanderlust. With such a fluid sense of geography in mind, we too can view a city's buildings as mountains – inside, outside and up on the roof. When we do so, we perceive wildness in the most unlikely of places.

Hours after the birders have made their descent, the bar on the forty-second floor beneath fills with the mingled sound of champagne flutes. The lunchtime gaggle migrates in from the banks and investment houses to chew over market sentiment and strips of rare beef drenched in tarragon mayonnaise. Across ponds of crisp white tablecloths, diners toss titbits of information between themselves about the next big kill: news of a promising territory, gossip over the whereabouts of a weak and shaky bottom line. In there, the world is flat and theirs to conquer. Outside, the wind chooses a new direction.

## A LOFTY POSITION

A panorama of a metropolis at height makes a mockery of our sense that it is an aloof island, that it has no physical connection to the wild, that the pull of the moon has no power over its rivers. With our feet on the ground, our bearings are off; we don't remember the city is always a place in a greater scheme, one landscape on an extremely extensive map, an environment built upon and shaped by geological processes millions of years old. We rarely consider the history of the rocks in which the foundations of our skyscrapers are rooted.

When I take time to climb so high above the city, I'm often surprised to see the treetops of a woodland or park that, when earthbound, I tend to think of as too far away to visit. And it is as pleasing to notice how these glimpses of nature look so fluid – streams and trickles and spats and droplets in varying shades of green, liquid pouring in and around the grooves and gaps within our structures and systems.

Take up a lofty position atop a soaring block, and the city dweller's world is no longer defined by the architectural outline of a development spree. It becomes a city, compressed by, beaten back by sky. It is where we catch a view of the sunlight, not as a laser of light off a pane of glass but as a watery haze that muddles with

the colour of clouds, a luminous presence that
accentuates the contours and edges of landmarks
near and far all at the same time.

## THE SOUND OF SILENCE

And then there's the sound of the wind: a whisper,
a whistle, a howl that whips around the ears. It is the
same wind-silence of the mountain, a wind that muffles
all other noise – cars, commerce, church bells – and makes
you feel quite alone. A sound of silence that takes us
off-road and wraps us in the wildness of the moment.

In that moment, we can contemplate that this silence
is the same as long ago – the same sound that blew across
the ice sheets and formed the cold tundra landscape
that characterized the spot of Earth I now inhabit. It
is the same sound that the explorer has always heard
as he stands at the peak, still with a connection to the
base camp he set out from but with his gaze fixed on
an entirely new sight line, a fresh point of interest way
off out in the distance.

# Watch the
# **Birds Move**

High up above, over rooftops and high-rises, down railway tracks, across grassy glades and the canopies of trees, the birds move, their choreography at odds with the pace on the streets below, our frantic human jazz. We can easily spot them; ascending the sky as if it possessed a steep rollercoaster, soaring, in swift flight, or simply drifting. Fleeing in cloudbursts, straggly lines, alone or in pairs – the city's birds move with grace, at complete ease with the air.

Watch as they move with the breath of the Earth, manoeuvring to the breeze, employing its force. Starlings migrate at night, when the air is calm and cool. Raptors seize on the currents rising up the sides of tall buildings to reach higher altitudes. Skeins of geese position wing tips in precisely the place to catch an upward gust, mastering aerodynamics to conserve energy in flight.

## SWEET SURRENDER

It took a testing time in my life for me to open my eyes to the birds, to the beauty of the forms they create as they criss-cross the skies, to how watching them could soothe. It was summer, and a boiling Saturday. Blazing with fury, I'd cut loose from the house to the public gardens nearby with the intention of lying defeated in the grass. Phone off, headphones in – I intended to settle there for an evening of cathartic self-pity.

About me, oak leaves fluttered; the grass was lithe enough to hide lovers. In a cloudless sky, the birds made long curvatures of flight, while others journeyed from tree to tree in rhythmic flits. I spotted a lone bird and followed its airborne undulations. I surrendered my breath, slowing its pace to this mood, trying to inhale and exhale in tune with the swaying treetops.

The sensation of the grass, and how it tickled my calves, registered in my thoughts. I became aware of my skull, heavy in my hands. I saw how my body belonged to this moment: part of the Earth, but with a physical weight completely insignificant to it. Just as a soil molecule rests in a garden – a minuscule grain of the whole.

## THE THEATRE OF FLIGHT

Observing birds in flight like this, it can be sobering to ponder the millions of years of evolution behind these easy movements; since *Archaeopteryx*, the earliest feathered being on record, manoeuvred around the planet with its rudimentary bird body. Lying there in the grass, I felt privileged to have a front row seat to this theatre of flight, to be treated to a live demo of one of natural history's many fascinating achievements.

As I watched, I began to wonder at what the birds see as they soar our city skies, whether our world looks as balletic to them. I guessed they'd seen too many of us pounding pavements with more speed than is necessary.

Tipping our eyes to the skies can remind us that it is possible to invest more grace in our own terra firma gestures. We tend to assume agitated postures in tedious queues for coffee, or waiting for a delayed bus. We run for trains when there's no pressing reason; dart to a laid-back weekend brunch engagement. Minds react to the physical haste by always wanting to be where we're not. In this heightened state, our thoughts charge our feet. When overwrought, it is common to expend more energy than is needed on our own physical endeavours.

But walking can be such a pleasurable act, an ability in which millions of years of evolution has been invested. Over this time, our ancestors perfected the act of putting one foot in front of the other and made the transition from climbing trees to fully bipedal roaming.

## SIMPLY GLIDE

Watching birds as they swoop and soar, I'm reminded that it is not only possible, but that we are similarly programmed for such mellowness in our actions. Feet are highly sensitive tools, capable of communicating the physical stress we are placing on ourselves from one moment to the next. Nature has designed feet with hundreds of thousands of nerves and wired them up to a complex neuromechanical feedback mechanism that signals how much pressure to place on our joints. Like an in-built therapist, our feet will alert us to when we need to slow down.

To 'hear' this natural process at work, which is underway at all times, we must make a mental note of the simple physical action of placing our feet on the Earth. How does the ball of your foot feel as it engages with the ground, or the heel? And how appropriate is the pace of movement to the purpose of it?

City life often demands pace – but not every second of it. Let your feet tell you when to speed up. It will be less often than you expect. There are occasions to be as graceful as the birds. Just like them, there are times to make haste, and there are times to simply glide on an indiscernible current.

# The Art of
# **Looking**

I've always loved an alternative map. The type that you can pick up from a café counter or notice hanging on the wall in the stylish home of a friend. In these maps, the city is illustrated only with the whereabouts of one kind of store or landmark – its independent bookshops, vintage clothes stores, curving rivers or places of historical interest, often drawn out of proportion so they pop up from the streets.

Among my favourites is a literary map of London, a hand-drawn typographical illustration created with names of characters from the pages of novels based in the city, plotted on the bits they most liked to roam or call home. Then there's an abstract expression of the iconic colourful tube map, which replaces its rectilinear geography with wild wiggles, tight loops and arching freer-form lines.

These maps remind me that the geography of the metropolis can be personal, unlike the standard versions that detail every street. And they are the mental maps we create as we explore our environment, subconsciously building a picture of the city from the bars, canals, buildings and districts we love – memories that are so crucial because they make a place come alive.

When we take note of the physical reality of the environment, it allows us to appreciate it deeply and develop a strong sense of home and belonging, because our surroundings become both familiar and distinct to us. This allows the metropolis to be vivid and memorable, rather than an overwhelming and alienating sprawl.

But we can miss opportunities to foster a sense of home, a visual connection to our surroundings, when we spend train journeys staring at screens and navigate streets with our eyes fixed on the blue dot of the map that shows us if we're going the right way. When we do this, we prevent the city from speaking to us in a way we've never before heard. When we do this, we prevent ourselves from looking a place squarely in the eye.

## MASTERING THE ART OF LOOKING

All that's tough about mastering the art of looking is being mindful of the need to do it. Being at liberty to walk, cycle or take advantage of buses or trains in the city makes that possibility to connect visually so much easier.

Public transport allows us the freedom to look that I sorely missed in the country, where a set of wheels was as fundamental to survival as a set of waterproofs. When I lived rurally, there was no question of not taking the car anywhere I wanted to go – the doctor, the supermarket, the post office – unless I had three days spare to romp the cliff paths to my destination. Being the sole driver in the family, I was always at the wheel, my focus fixed straight ahead as I tried to navigate single-track lanes while the stunning scenery passed me by.

As I battled with these quaint but treacherous roads, I realized how my eyes were so much freer to roam when being carried to my destination. Public transport may not always, I admit, be relaxing, but on my return to the city I appreciated it so much more. Where I used to save train journeys to reply to messages stored up in my phone, I now gaze out of the window to absorb the contours of a skyline and all the life contained there; giving myself a chance to revel in the urban landscape.

Working alone most of the time, I get a kick seeing the office blocks beside the railway tracks on my journeys. They have these generous windows through which I can see smart looking people talking over tables, reams of paper and coffee cups. Then there are the swathes of flats, whether it's those luxuriously glossy developments or brutalist 1960s' estates – common to them all are the balconies so politely stacked upon one another. I love to see how each is adorned, with burgeoning plant pots, picnic tables or mini washing lines bearing laundry to be dried by the sun.

## COLOURING THE MAP

Walking offers sensory connection to the ground.
Our feet note the undulations, where a path is steep
or sloping. If we travel the same routes continually,
our knowledge of the street becomes intimate – like
anticipating which steps on a staircase will creak.

But fostering familiarity isn't its only strength. Walking
allows us to rise above the single-minded efficiency of
a navigation system. Walking a city, where commerce,
history, beauty are packed in tight like blades of grass,
allows us to annotate the dull lines of a physical map
with full colour. We can look at a street name and know
that this is where the house fronts are painted in pastels
or where the ancient river runs buried beneath the
tarmac. We can continually embellish our own mental
maps with new details. We become both at home and
aware of the fact that the city is an open-ended order
that's forever providing us with a fresh picture.

# Learn to be
# Optimistic

A friend once told me she saw optimism as a gift. Often it can be much harder to be positive about life, and easier to dwell on negative thoughts. Emotional resilience, one that gives us strength to retain that sense of optimism about the world, to nurture a positive outlook, is the best spiritual skill we can teach ourselves. It is also much-needed in the testing times of the cities we call home.

On the weekend, the city's joyful and relaxing nature seems accessible. As we meet friends for drinks, explore a new district, amble around historic sites along with the tourists, we connect to it without the stress of the working week. But Monday to Friday the city can feel like a beast, and one that brings out the worst in humanity.

So often this is down to the uncivilized battle of the daily commute. As we fight our way to work with millions of others, all trying to get somewhere punctually, it is par for the course to come across what feels like inconsiderate, unthinking people. At these times, urban life feels full of people so consumed with their own agendas that they have no time for politeness.

Not only is this frustrating, these experiences also make us believe that mental peace and spiritual balance cannot exist in cities, or is near on impossible to retain. And when we regularly encounter behaviour we don't like, it can make us feel less compassionate and forgiving.

## EXTENDING COMPASSION

It's important, however, not to allow these moments to make us feel jaded about city life as a whole. The default feeling that the faceless, aggressive, overcrowded metropolis makes all who dwell in it self-centred is not only a skewed view of how cities – and people – really are, it is also no good for anxiety levels.

Extending compassion at times of intensely irritating encounters with rudeness or angry traffic is easier when we consider our own experience. I expect very few of us would say the city has made us blind to others. No one believes the city makes him or her impatient and selfish but we readily jump to those conclusions about everyone else.

When we ourselves do things in a rush, we know our excuses for it: 'I didn't see the person also going for that seat'; 'If I don't cram on to this train, there's no way I'm getting to the 9am meeting on time' – and so on. We should try to remember that commuting is just as stressful for everyone else; it doesn't make them who they are, any more than it makes us who we are.

## THIS TOO SHALL PASS . . .

What we must also remember is that these experiences are fleeting. Instead of clinging to a negative interaction from the morning rush hour, allowing it to dictate how we feel about our day in the city, we can teach ourselves to experience the metropolis in a way that is not solely shaped by our own emotions, but one that embraces one of the core principles of mindfulness: impermanence.

The idea of impermanence teaches that life is essentially ephemeral. Nothing lasts – whether the moment is good, bad, beautiful or ugly, it will all pass. The city is no exception in its nature – all its sights, sounds, movement and interactions are part of a constant flow. That constant flow, of all kinds of moments, is a more true and realistic interpretation of how the city functions day-to-day.

You only have to think of the tables at a busy café to appreciate this notion of city life as a river of experience – people come and go continually, to meet with friends, or talk business, to read a newspaper or watch the world go by. Or notice how a crowd moves through a railway station like a flock of birds, making only an indistinct impression on the eyes before it disappears as quickly as it appeared.

Or you might remember having seen a gang of old men meeting under trees to play chess, children sailing boats on the pond of a public garden, the gentle mood of those browsing the riverside bookstall – the kind of moment you might have had the time, and the headspace, to enjoy on a weekend. Bringing these sights and memories to the forefront of the mind, we're able to contextualize that which tests us about the city, and imagine it as a place of just as much ease and tranquillity.

So, perhaps someone pushes ahead of you in the queue for the bus or sighs at you for taking too long at the ticket machine – but just as quickly the scene will change to one in which you may observe beauty or people in quiet, unhurried enjoyment.

# Embrace
# Chaos

For a period of time I lived under a hectic flight
path. The planes skimmed so close to our rooftop
you could read the livery on the aircraft's underbelly.
During summers, when holiday traffic was at its peak,
I would awake at 4am to the roar of planes approaching
the city's largest airport. With sleep a distant dream,
I would instead count the seconds of skyward peace
between each plane – often around 14 seconds.

The nightly racket never disturbed my other half.
He was never wrenched from sleep to the sound of his
head being microwaved. But the dear old flat had other
issues. The Victorian floorboards were worn so thin
that we could hear the bachelor who lived below – the

sound of his cutlery scraping the final mouthfuls of dinner from his plate, the whir of his washing machine, his incessant smoker's cough, his sex life, everything. And he could hear us, which included, he told me one day (much to my horror), our bathroom visits.

It was awkward for us all. Whenever I bumped into him on the street I apologized for our existence, and despite us doing everything we could to live quietly, he often complained to our landlord. But life is a noisy business, and though we tried to skate around like water boatmen, there was only so much we could do to mitigate our impact upon him. But it is how cities are. Wherever we city dwellers are located, we live our days like the filling in a huge triple-decker sandwich; with stuff going on above, below and to either side.

## CULTIVATE A POSITIVE ATTACHMENT

In the extreme, noise pollution can be awful for our health. Humans are not passive recipients of stressful environmental conditions. In striving to cope, our blood pressure rises, as do our heart rates. Anxiety is also an effect, among a long list of others. Nevertheless, there are plenty like my other half who are better able to deal with the soundtrack of the city, who even find it comforting or inspiring. It seems the difference is in the way these people perceive the constant chatter of the metropolis, its sirens and traffic and indecipherable hubbub. For these easy-going types, noise represents the potential of the city, all the characters and lives it contains.

Cultivating a positive attachment to the chaos can excite the imagination. Noise represents the fascinating energy of the city; all of its human journeys, its possibilities. Whether it's a bus or a café or on the street, overhearing fragments of sentences here and there gives little insights into other lives, like messages tied to balloons that have been released into the air. In these fragments you will hear a city that can speak fluently in more languages than you can name.

There's something humbling and grounding about hearing voice after voice after voice. It can stop you getting too wrapped up in your own life story, or the seeming magnitude of it. But positive associations like this can also help us build resilience to the intensely irritating stuff, like the neighbours in the apartment above who are always screaming at one another, or the nocturnal yapping of dogs.

## IT'S NOTHING PERSONAL...

The trick is to avoid perceiving noise as having been sent to disrupt you personally. It is easy to allow unwelcome noise to set us on a downward spiral that can swiftly carry us to anger at the neighbours, which builds into fury that they are completely inconsiderate of you, and next, to a feeling of frustration that your own circumstances mean you are forced to live so close to everyone else, rather than the quiet house on a prairie.

When we accept a particular noise as a basic fact, when we do not spin it into a web of our own emotions, we take control over it and train our mind to apply more productive and forgiving thoughts. Maybe that means hoping the neighbours survive their troubles, or maybe you choose to believe that the reason they don't approach you in the hall to apologize for their disruptive behaviour is that they're acutely embarrassed. By simply developing awareness of how our own thought process contributes to the stress we feel in noisy circumstances, we give ourselves an invaluable tool, one that gifts us a sense of control over, and distance from, the volume of chaos when we need it most.

# The Joy
## of Small Living

There is a children's book by Leo Lionni called *The Biggest House in the World*, a story with which many urban dwellers could empathize. It tells the story of a young snail who wishes to have the largest shell that any snail has ever possessed. But when his father hears of his son's ambition, he tells him the tragic tale of another snail with the same dream.

This snail gave everything he could to grow the most outlandish shell possible. The colossal shell drew admiration from all the other garden creatures, but lay so heavy upon him that eventually he could no longer move. Unable to travel to his food, the poor snail faded away until nothing remained but the shell itself. 'Some things are better small,' the wise father warned the young mollusc. 'Keep your house light and easy to carry.'

If you live in a city, it's likely you've dreamed the same dream. Cramming the boundless landscape of our possessions into tiny apartments is just the way it is, and with every year that passes, it seems the monthly pay packet affords ever fewer square metres. During my most recent flat hunt, I came across a kitchen so minuscule the fridge had to be stored in the living room, and one apartment with so little floor space its occupants were forced to hang their bikes over the bathtub.

Being cooped up like battery hens can make us a little bit resentful of our cities. It can create a constant longing for more space, and often the only way to achieve that is to earn much more money, or live so far out in the suburbs that you're no longer part of a vibrant scene. Without the prospect of ever possessing a garden, or room to put a dining table, even, you begin to wonder if clinging to the city is worth it.

None of this is good for our sense of belonging. If the idea of home is always a dream as we move from one apartment to the next every couple of years, our capacity to mentally settle, to feel at one in a city, is hindered. But while there is little we can do to fight the economics of metropolitan real estate, we can use mindfulness to help us challenge those feelings.

## FREEDOM TO ROAM

As the young snail's father knew, not everything our heart desires is wise, and chasing our ideals doesn't always bring happiness. Small homes offer us a greater opportunity for adventure. Freedom to roam is our home, not the walls that surround us. Weekends are not invested in regrouting the bathroom, as the proud homeowner might, but in exploring and communing with the myriad experiences the city offers. The theatres, cinemas and bookshops are extensions of our living rooms; the parks are our gardens; the restaurants, serving cuisine from every country, are our windows into the world beyond.

Diminutive homes come with diminutive responsibilities. We have fewer walls to paint, fewer shelves to dust, fewer possessions to maintain. When we're uncertain how long we'll be in any one place, we tend not to accumulate as quickly or as much as our friends with the huge pad in the countryside – there's no point buying furniture that will be too cumbersome to lug to the next flat and may not even fit through the front door.

We become ascetic about material matters. Without the luxury of space, we question whether the tempting object in the window is worth the shelf space it would occupy. Objects feel like a burden. We prune wardrobes for anything that's not needed. We stay light, we do not cling to the idea of possessions. And as the Buddha says, 'When one does not cling, one does not feel agitated.'

## A SENSE OF PLACE

Home is a very spiritual idea that means something different to everyone. The conventional idea of the perfect home is the imagery of magazines: a beautifully designed and perfectly proportioned space. But the spiritual idea of home is less tangible. The *feeling* of home can reach us through our eyes, our noses, our taste and touch. For me, it can be invoked by the soft air and lush green hills of the countryside that I grew up in. But for others it could be the smell of freshly baked bread, making a recipe from an old family cookbook, sharing a meal with friends with whom you have a long history.

Our little homes help us remain connected with these alternative ideas of belonging, and cities – such treasure troves of experiences – allow us to cultivate those more philosophical interpretations. The more we roam, the more we experience of the world, the greater chance we have of feeling rooted, at one, across a greater number of its landscapes, cultures, people. Our shells may be small, but we are the adventurers who are free to taste all of the city's pleasures.

# Embrace
# Resourcefulness

It can sometimes seem that only the wealthy have the right to belong in the city. Urban places are home to some of the richest people on the planet, who are able to participate in all that the metropolis offers – feast in its priciest restaurants, dwell in homes with the spectacular vistas illustrated in the tourist brochures.

Money buys the freedom to navigate a city in style, to experience only the glossiest bits, like the cab that whizzes you to your destination so fast you only see the glitzy lights, never the grit. When an average income barely covers your rent, let alone much in the way of social fun, it can feel as if to take joy in a city we must buy into the pursuit of financial success, above all else.

But deep down we all know that happiness is a more complex psychology than living in luxury and comfort. It is best served when we stay in touch with our knowledge that, however buoyant the bank balance, spiritual values such as compassion, generosity and togetherness are those that truly nourish. Similarly, finding ways to live with fewer material possessions, being content with and taking care of what we have, is another mindful, nurturing goal.

## LEARN A NEW SKILL

Buying what we need (or think we need) is the easiest option in time-poor lives. But it is more expensive, and nowhere near as rewarding as choosing to live a little more resourcefully – growing, making, mending, recycling and upcycling.

Most of us don't have time to become a fully self-sufficient human, to cultivate our own food and make all of our own clothes. But it isn't necessary to be so evangelical. Adopting an attitude of resourcefulness in one area of your life is an enriching endeavour.

Urban places are fantastically fertile environments in which to learn skills that can help us achieve this. Short courses, workshops and drop-in sessions teaching techniques in anything you desire – from DIY to textiles to baking bread – are plentiful.

Consider their cost an investment, given that creative skills bequeath lifetime value. They also reconnect us with an ancestral aptitude for creation – how empowering to know how to fix up your broken bike, mend a much-loved outfit or grow herbs on a windowsill.

## CRAFT BEAUTIFUL THINGS

I've always thought that the artists and craftspeople of our cities are wonderful teachers of how to be thoughtful about our material possessions, and are a plentiful resource for inspiration.

Their work is often based on making the most of the materials they have to hand. They can imagine objects in new, exciting ways and craft what appears ugly or dull to everyone else into something beautiful – an arresting, colourful sculpture from recycled plastic bottles, garden planters from old car tyres.

Urban artists usually offer many opportunities all year round to view their work through showcases, exhibitions or pop-up events. Taking time to go along to these viewings and observe their inventiveness can encourage us to be similarly creative about the materials we have available.

At a fringe gardening festival one year, I joined a walking tour with a textile artist, who led us on a forage for plants in the hedgerows and waste grounds near her studio. She then showed us how to brew them, in saucepans, into natural material dyes. The experience opened my eyes to the versatility of plants, to how mysterious and deeply clever even the straggliest urban weed is.

I also once connected with an artist in my city who stitched exquisite patchwork quilts for people from the scraps of old clothing that they or their family had grown out of. These clothes had escaped being donated to the charity shop because of the memories they held but, with no useful purpose, were sitting redundant in a drawer. In an open studio demonstration, the artist showed how she turned these precious materials into the hexagonal pieces of a traditional bedspread, resurrecting a tapestry of family memories into an entirely new form. As much as anything else, we can admire the time and dedication that's required to make a success of a project like this.

For the craftsperson, even the novice, patience really is a virtue. And self-sufficiency skills bring us into physical contact with the present. Revel in the process and, for once, allow yourself to feel time is a tool, not an enemy. Find the meditative rhythm and quietude woven into this creative act – in the repeated looping of wool over needles, sanding a scuffed table or applying brushstrokes of fresh paint. It is soothing not only for the hands but for the mind, which becomes grounded in the peaceful sense of satisfaction intrinsic to the act of crafting beautiful things.

# Keep in Touch with
# Your Senses

Watching my toddler scoop up an object he has never before seen and turn it over in his hands, his eyes enlivened, intently taking it all in, reminds me how at one the mind and the hands should be. He could be looking at a nail file, a CD, a whisk, but there's wholeness to his actions nonetheless: a holy trinity of sensory exploration in which sight, touch and thought are completely in tune.

Feeling your way into the world like children do is a path to mindfulness. But to walk this path as an adult requires graft. I find that unless I consciously apply thought to a specific task, my limbs run on autopilot. As we grow older, as we get busier and more stressed out, we acquire deftness to our physicality, but we miss out on so many experiences of touch, experiences that can inform us about the shape of our environment.

It is crucial for our well-being, however, to try to retain that sense of wonder through sensory activities – and especially so in our urban surroundings, when we are often simply trying to get through a to-do list as efficiently as we can. When we do this, we see that feeling joy in a place isn't always just an intellectual pursuit, but one in which the hands can make contact with the city itself; its shape, texture, how warm or cool it is, how soft or hard.

For me, harvest time is one such opportunity since the city I live in produces wild food in abundance. The appeal of foraging is down to the repetitive, rhythmic action of picking from plants. It holds a hypnotic quality that allows the physical act to fill the moment. It is a time when my hands seem to lead my head, for a change – so that the only thought swimming through my mind is a respect for, and curiosity about, the complex chemistry that created the squidgy, auburn berry pinched between my fingers.

Not all cities are so well stocked in edible plants. But we can turn our hands to plenty of other pursuits that offer that same tangible connection to the urban environment, where the pleasure of a thing is registered by the fingers before the brain.

## TOUCHING A CITY'S HISTORY

The city is a trove of places that invite us to use our sense of touch as well as our eyes and ears. Botanic gardens and public parks are the obvious candidates. But fountains, sculptures and old brickwork can also offer us sensory pleasure. Running one's hand through a lively jet of water as it sparkles in the sunlight is a playful, childlike pleasure – and, moreover, this action of reaching out is instinctive to us to perform, bringing a simple enjoyment that can also ground us.

Every time I see a statue with some body part rubbed away by the hands of countless admirers, I'm reminded of how natural it is to us to want to reach out – so much so in the city of Verona that the authorities have been compelled to consign a bronze of Shakespeare's Juliet to a museum, because her right arm and breast have been damaged by the tens of thousands who have touched her in passing, to bring them good luck in love.

Placing a hand on a revered monument can make us more mindful of what it represents. But it can also remind us of the countless people who have stood in the same spot and taken spiritual solace from it, or of crucial moments that shaped a city's history. Touch is a way to *feel* this knowledge.

The historical places around our cities give us many opportunities to engage with ideas and people in a more contemplative way than if we had read the information in a book. Using our hands to experience them can connect us to people who may have lived before us, leading to a deeper understanding of that city's psychological identity.

## MESSAGES OF LOVE

Brushing my hands over the written messages and paintings that fill the Lennon Wall in Prague was one such time when I felt close to the persistence of the human spirit at a very significant time in the city's history. The wall has been named after the former Beatles singer – a hero of the pacifist youth of Central and Eastern Europe during the Communist era – since the 1980s, when people began writing his lyrics or those inspired by him upon it.

Despite repeated whitewashing of the messages of peace, the Communist police could never keep the wall clean; the next day it would again be adorned with poems and messages. At the time, the monument was a place for free speech and non-violent rebellion. Today it is still covered with messages of love, and if you run a finger slowly over the pen and paint marks, it is possible to feel the urgency of the hands that inscribed them.

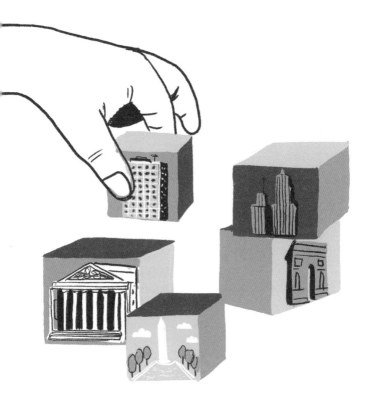

# Revel in
# Change

Where else can we be so well reminded of a city's powers of endurance and innovation than in its cemeteries? There is one in London that I have come to know well. Almost two hundred years in age, it is one of the oldest in the city, and the place where the souls of the city's long-gone notables of science, art, literature and industry rest in peace.

Among the tens of thousands of graves is that of Isambard Kingdom Brunel. Here, pilgrims pay homage to one of the country's most influential engineers, who designed the railways that connected cities for the first time and catapulted them to the industrial age.

But contemplating Brunel's legacy in this place now has a modern twist. His grave, and the cemetery itself, lie in the planned pathway of a major rail infrastructure project – newspaper gossip has been of a train tunnel that could be drilled mere metres below the tombs to support state-of-the-art tracks.

Brunel's grave is not at peace from the clickety-clack of progress. Change is always upon us, especially so in the metropolis, where nothing is ever considered finished. Whatever one has achieved, there's always someone with an alternative idea to improve upon it. In the city it's all change, all of the time.

## NEVER-ENDING RENEWAL

Always, the city is refining itself, and that change isn't necessarily for the better. We often berate the glitches of the metropolis, and curse any faults. Day to day, we keenly feel the problems of failure.

This continual adaptation – for better, for worse – means there's no sense of permanence in the city; no street or skyline remains as it is for long. This can make the city feel unknowable, maybe exhausting.

The nature of evolution of urban places, as it is in the natural world, is that it is a constant work in progress, and progress can be positive. When we take time to look back over decades, or centuries, we can more clearly understand how far we have come in some senses. An exhilarating charm may be taken from this never-ending renewal, one that can be inspirational in our own endeavours.

It tells us something new is always possible.

## AN EVOLVING PATCHWORK

One day, I set off to find Brunel's resting place – nestled in a landscape that undulates in places, like the waves you meet way out at sea. Everywhere cracked, sinking gravestones look adrift, as if they might, with just one heavy fall of rain, topple over and float away right out on to the street.

Winding pathways, monumental sycamore trees, leggy grass, meadowsweet blooming with frothy sociability; the place felt more garden than burial ground. Left to exist for almost two centuries, nature has thrived, thanks to its annual rhythm of resurrection.

The city beyond is just the same. Built layer upon layer, where new stands with old, where star-grazing skyscrapers teeter on the fringes of medieval marketplaces. A city is rarely built from scratch, but developed over the ages, and that is often what's captivating about it. This patchwork of past, present and future makes cities imperfect beasts. But it also makes them experts in tenacity.

It is in historic architecture that we can take comfort in this talent for steadfastness, when we see a building or streets that have evaded the enthusiasm of a modern planner's pen. As we place our feet in the worn grooves of their ageing steps, we can remember our urban ancestors, and wonder at what has been overcome since their time.

# SPIRIT OF THE CITY

As we witness the next generation of buildings rising from the ground, we can discern a spirit of the city that is forever changing, forever trying to keep pace with the future. It keeps us mindful of the fact that cities are so often places where its people, at one time, have rebuilt ruins and overcome destruction.

They are also places where bright minds have invented solutions. Humankind has achieved much from creative collaborations that have flourished in cities across the world – think of Florence and Venice as the hotbed of the Renaissance, or Athens, where in the fifth century BCE a system of 'rule by the people' formed the foundation of democracy.

Imagine what is set to come in the future, as places such as Singapore, Vancouver and Munich have begun working on solutions to lower their carbon footprint and raise standards of liveability. Far from the concerns of Brunel these may be, but perhaps driven by the spirit of visionary thinking that the great man would have recognized.

# Find Beauty
# in Form

Asked to compare our home cities with a work of art, many of us might liken their composition to a hectic abstract painting, a mess of lines and shapes; a scramble of streets, buildings and neighbourhoods; a picture of movement and activity.

The visual complexity of the cityscape can give a place a powerful energy that fires us and inspires us. But with so much mental stimulation, it can also feel as though there's not much that's soothing about the urban environment. Simplicity isn't a founding design principle for nothing: simple things are pleasing to the eye. Bombarded with too much visual stimuli, we feel tired and overwhelmed as we try to make sense of what we are looking at.

A beautiful form is, therefore, a refuge: an elegant structure or a minimalist arrangement of shapes provides respite from a chaotic environment. In craftsmanship, we have the pathway to a better mind state – it is why tea sipped from a handmade mug is more restorative than one taken from a polystyrene cup, why the glimpse of a spider's web beaded with dew feels like a gift.

But artistry is a common feature of our cityscapes, too. Think of the form contained in the architecture of a bridge, the order in a series of ornate spires or the geometry of a string of colonnades. Bringing focus to snapshots of rhythm and order is restful for a busy brain.

## LANDMARK ARCHITECTURE

Both visually arresting and meditative to explore, cities are usually home to imaginatively designed modern buildings. For me, those constructed with vast quantities of glass, high ceilings, minimal interiors and masses of natural light are particularly charming, providing a sense of space you aren't afforded on busy streets.

Reykjavik's Harpa concert hall is like this. Structured as a tilted cliff face, its walls have been built with multiple hexagonal glass tubes, studded with coloured and mirrored panes, as well as a mirrored ceiling. Inspired by Iceland's volcanic geology, it has been designed to filter, refract and fragment the light.

Public libraries can be similarly commanding architectural monuments, with the added benefit that they are also quiet oases. New York Public Library is a majestic landmark combining hand-carved classical details, vast reading rooms and one of the largest un-columned interior spaces in the world, while Copenhagen's Black Diamond library floats on a raised ribbon of glass that offers panoramic views of the surrounding waterfront, wave-like balconies and a cascading fountain to fill the space with the calming sound of water.

Many cities have their own gems just like these, designed for those seeking solace from the intensity and noise of the streets.

## A SPIRITUAL ARTISTRY

Cities are not homogeneous. Often, they're a patchwork of unique districts that each possesses a mood, culture and way of life that are characteristic of that place – and thus a heart and soul that is enriching to be immersed in. These neighbourhoods, you could say, have a spiritual artistry.

Vibe cannot be manufactured overnight. It is created by a collective memory of the people who have lived and worked in a place, and generated over years by multiple forces and hundreds of individuals. It is the unconscious product of the choices, whims and ideas of these successive generations.

In these neighbourhoods, we find an eclectic mix of stores, not global chains; a diverse community – socially, economically and culturally – and creatives who bring life to the streetscape. We can shop in delis run by the same family for decades, ramble in record shops and nose about a long-established market. It is in these places that the city shows itself to be made up of many personalities.

A vibrant neighbourhood is a precious thing, and we should take delight in its authenticity. Success like this often leaves a place vulnerable to rising property values, quickly pricing out the community that made it such a textured place to be.

Relish those neighbourhoods you come across that retain a heart that still beats strongly, because they tell a story of a very special kind of history, of communities with deep roots in a very particular patch of the Earth. A captivating vibe cannot be conjured any other way – at least, not in a way that's convincing. So seek out those soulful districts, and take joy in the fact that, there, it still feels true.

# Musical
## Discoveries

Music is as instinctive to humans as walking is to a newborn foal. It is a universal pleasure. Even babies show sensitivity to rhythm, are captivated by it – a capacity for enjoyment that begins in the womb. When we hear music, dopamine – the 'pleasure chemical' – is triggered, as well as emotional and intellectual responses. Recurring sounds, notes meshing harmoniously or the repetition of melody stimulates our brains, makes us happy and induces many other emotions besides.

Music happens where people meet, so a city is often blessed with a mixed musical scene, with hundreds of live gigs underway on any one night. For many cities, that scene is part of its unique character. Cities can be synonymous with classical jazz, gospel, rhythm and blues or brass band street music – traditions that tell of a place's unique history. Discovering new genres is as gratifying as hearing those we know. Living in a city, with its host of musical communities, we have much opportunity to journey pleasure pathways we've never before tried.

## SPOILT FOR CHOICE

We also have a variety of venue choices, each creating a discrete experience or mood. You might choose to hear a heavy metal group in a concert venue with thousands of others, a symphony orchestra in an ancient cathedral or a lone soul singer in a little-known bar. The venue, as well as the way it shapes our participation, is intrinsic to the kind of meditative adventure live music offers. One reason is that these venues will sculpt acoustics, and may even be designed to amplify or enhance them. Music halls may be structured with a ceiling of umbrella vaults that create low reverberation, ideal for hearing romantic ballads, while other venues may have padded rooms that allow the listener to better distinguish the strings or brass instruments of an orchestra.

Awareness that physical spaces can complement sound like this establishes a deeper connection with the music, and reminds us that sometimes an architect has given thought to heightening our aural, as well as our optical, senses. Even if they have not, it is enlivening to conceive music as a physical being that has weight in the air, that weaves about the room serpent-like, as real and present as light or shade.

Seen this way, we immerse ourselves in the performance and can be fully present with it. Listening becomes an active rather than a passive event. We can explore the tone and rhythm entering our ears. An ability to read music or play an instrument doesn't preclude us from doing this; it is a personal interaction. Nobody is going to quiz you on the technical aspects afterwards. So be as inquisitive as possible about what you hear, and allow it to entertain you.

You can discern if the tune appears to you to drift or soar. You might try to identify whether the beat is fast or slow. Music is designed to provoke a mood, so be alert to the emotions it is rousing; it could be nostalgia, excitement or awe. Your feeling might be what the composer intended, but you are at liberty to respond how you want to; there are no 'right' answers, no matter what critics claim.

## MADE TO HEAR MUSIC

Live performance is more arresting than listening to a recording. Being in the presence of talented artists is inspiring, and the communality of the enjoyment is meditative because it is cheering to see others share your passion for a piece. And that passion can be shared among a diverse audience, an audience of differing cultures, religions and languages – the kind of audience you find in a multicultural metropolis.

This is one of music's transcendental qualities. It can reach beyond social constructs and specificities and speak direct to the soul. Hence, even the music of a particular culture, one that tells a unique story of that community, has power to move those who've never experienced that history. In this kind of music, we are reminded that, though we are each on an individual path, feelings of heartbreak, loss, joy and bliss are common to us all.

As an audience member, we can empathize with the emotional experience of others. We also become part of something; from the first note to the last, music has the capacity to bind us into a temporary society. It may only hold us tight together for a short while, before we disperse again on to the streets, like a cloud bursting into shower, forever going our separate ways. But perhaps we do so feeling a little more human, feeling part of a species – one whose ears were made to hear music.

# Through the Eyes
## of Others

There was an old cherry tree that grew beside the last house we lived in before we had our first baby. I could never work out how it had endured for so long there, squashed up against the house – so close, in fact, that its elderly branches scratched against the kitchen window, splaying its gnarled twigs in an undignified fashion over the panes of glass, making it look from indoors like an abstract painting.

It was during the spring that it seemed to rise above its cramped living conditions and overcome the ugliness of its lot in life alongside a fence lined with rubbish bins. It revelled instead in its cloudbursts of faint pink blossom, so effusive they could be seen from the end of the street. On those first warm days of the year, when the windows were open, I'd be forever finding its dainty petals all over our tiny flat, continually brushing them from the cooker top or scooping them from the carpet as the breeze blew them in.

The cleaning job didn't bother me. I had much affection for that tree. Over our years there, it had become part of our landscape. Its spring blossom reconciled my eyes to a street I too often hurried to disconnect from, whose oppressive feel I'd erase with the slam of a front door at the end of a long day. But in staring out at those flowers while waiting for the kettle to boil, I'd marvel at the tenacity of the bees that had battled around the thundering traffic to find their way to the tree's nectar. And then I'd find myself gazing out at the world beyond its branches, appreciating the details of the street life I'd usually barely register. In this sense it was like a portal into the present, drawing my attention to the colours in the slabs of sky peeping between houses and in the buds rearing from window boxes.

# LIFE BEFORE SUNDIALS

The cherry tree also reminded me that the mood of the Earth was a presence in the urban. The tree breathed, flowered, fed the bees, slept in wintertime – this unassuming life cycle ran to an ancient time so easy to overlook in busy places. And this ancient time, in the tiniest glimpses of greenery, in the gaps between the bricks and railway lines and chain-link fences, continued to pulse away with a rhythm quite distinct from the tick-tock pace that governed our lives; the same way that it had for billions of years before the invention of sundials. Before we humans organized our days according to hours, minutes and seconds.

Looking out at the street beyond, during these times, I'd notice the elderly retirees appearing at the bus stop, surfacing after the rush of workers heading for their morning trains – alone or in pairs, they'd stand waiting patiently for the bus to the high street with shopping bags and walking sticks in hand, their own harried morning commutes now behind them. Such characters, we forget, are so much a part of our neighbourhoods. But when we work and socialize with people just like us, with our own 'tribe' if you like, it can be easy to lose sight of the demographic diversity of the city.

## RETIREMENT IN THE CITY

But there are 500 million urbanites over the age of 60 across the globe, and the United Nations predicts that number will reach one billion within the next decade. Not all of these people are in cities by choice, of course. And there are many for whom the dynamic and socially progressive opportunities of cities are impossible to access. Equally, there are many who choose to remain in the metropolis for positive reasons, even though they are free from the constraints of a job. And their perspectives on what the metropolis can bring a person in old age can remind us all about the advantages of urban life.

I once interviewed a man in his eighties who, on retirement from his career as a civil engineer, swapped his acres of fields, sheep and a four-bedroom cottage in the country for a small apartment in a vast estate that surrounds the Barbican Arts Centre – one of the largest performing arts centres in Europe. We'd met to discuss his prizewinning balcony garden, but our chat drifted to his love for his city existence, made with days spent singing with a Gregorian chanting group, and attending some two hundred concerts a year. For this gentleman, the city gave his days height and depth, and the ability to eat Italian food whenever he fancied. The city was the best chance, he believed, to commune with people and places in a variety of ways.

It was a reminder of the value of urban networks, and how fortunate we are, as city dwellers, to be able to curate a multitude of communities that reflect our passions and support our well-being – especially vital for those who live alone. Opportunities to join a local interest group, take an evening class or build good relationships with our neighbours are replete in urban places, and among many simple actions we can take to lay the foundations of a long, happy urban existence.

# Make
# Soul Memories

If someone described you as a *carpe diem* person, it's
pretty likely you would take it as a huge compliment.
Most of us aspire to making every day count, even
though it isn't always achievable, given the need to
pay bills or fetch groceries. And we city dwellers, with
so much choice, arguably possess a wide array of tools
to live every day as if it is our last.

You might not think that living the *carpe diem* life
has anything to do with freeing yourself of FOMO:
the 'fear of missing out'. But I wonder if the act of
bringing moments to life has less to do than we assume
with tearing around mopping up all the gigs, exhibitions,
concerts and pop-up cocktail bars on offer.

## MAKING MOMENTS REAL

A very long time ago, when I was a teenager, I read Arthur Golden's *Memoirs of a Geisha*, and still fondly recall one of the last scenes of the story in which the Chairman, an elderly Japanese man near the end of his life, is taking his last walk through New York's Central Park. He stops at a pathway through the pine trees and, hand on his cane, eyes closed, breathes in the scent. It transports him to the pines that grew on the street in Osaka where he lived as a child. Golden writes, 'Sometimes,' he sighed, 'I think the things I remember are more real than the things I see.'

Like those Central Park trees, moments must be allowed space to expand in the heart. 'Breathe it in' is a phrase we hear when confronted with something spectacular but, while trite, it remains truthful. Our experiences are only the beginnings of meaningful memories: to find the moment still with you years hence, it must be seen, smelt, felt and heard. Ticking off a cultural to-do list doesn't guarantee that, or make our lives feel more real. For me, *carpe diem* means bringing your soul to the present, to let the rare beauty of the present moment imprint upon you.

But sometimes, seizing a moment doesn't require much mental effort – it can happen all on its own. When I lived away from the city for a while, and missed it terribly, I found myself remembering incidental happenings. I thought of the accordion player, that day by the river, who broke from his set list to play a lullaby for my crying baby son as I rocked him on a nearby bench. I thought of hugging a friend tightly on the station platform late at night, drunk and sorry for our pointless row, as people whizzed on and off trains. In all those years of my life in the city, I had been effortlessly *feeling* experiences I had not planned, forgetting so much else that I had.

## LET THE MOMENT HAPPEN

Lingering, or the ability to just be in a place, is a wonderful way to connect with the new and spontaneous experiences of city life. In this mood, we release the need for control and let the moment happen, like letting a shoreline wave wash over your bare feet. Public spaces, where you can observe the rhythm of pedestrians going about their lives and the creativity of street theatre or performance art, are rich with opportunities to experience the quality of moments without any time pressure, and elevate us from the deep furrows of our individual perspectives.

Rest on the steps of a cathedral for a while and feel the camaraderie of a tour group eating sandwiches, enthusing over the sights they've seen that morning, how they speak with fondness for your home city. Stand for a time on a busy pedestrian bridge and notice how even though each person's journey and destination is unique, their footsteps make the same sound. Or sit in a busy piazza and notice the coming and going, the handful of human stories you can read in the figures milling around – the young couple pledging their love by the fountain; the lively teens whizzing about on their bikes; the lone lady feeding bread to the pigeons.

Notice how the scene changes, and effortlessly; how these presences emerge then evaporate. Notice how tuning in to this makes you see a pace in the city that is the opposite of hurried. Rather, this pace is more akin to a poem, in which each character you observe possesses its own line, makes its own sound, its own shape on the page, represents its own truth.

People watching is a window into a softer reality of metropolitan life; one in which all we need is a bit of time to understand or feel it. Sometimes, to simply stand still is how we might best find joy in movement.

# A Home for
# Introverts

The last time I tried public speaking, it was a disaster.
I was taking part in an event for London-lovers, and had
been invited to take the stage as one of ten experts on the
city, to give a talk about why I was so passionate about
it. My ode was on London's natural world, but despite
all the convictions I had on this subject, the hundreds
in the audience went home none the wiser to them.

I was a shambles. My voice shook throughout, and
I barely took a breath for several sides of A4, racing
through my speech without glancing up, just trying to
get it over with. Hearing all the accomplished, confident
speakers before me, who talked with such eloquence
without notes, I had become increasingly nervous –

the three shots of rum I'd sunk before the doors opened having done zilch for my courage.

On the train home, I felt acutely embarrassed, a failure in the shadow of the other speakers, who'd had such an easy confidence on stage, as if they were doing nothing more intimidating than chatting to their mothers. But I also thought that, as an introvert who likes to remain quiet in a city that never stops talking, it was surreal to be thrust alone under a spotlight, to the sound of silence, to the glare of so many eyes fixating solely upon me.

The noise of the city is a comfort when you're a quiet one. While the city is most definitely an extrovert, and therefore makes a natural home for similarly self-assured and fearless characters, it is just as comfortable for the shy, for those who like to swim soft and silent in the undercurrent of this chaos.

I began to think about all those other urban dwellers just like me, who have a tendency to introversion. Ill-advised public speaking engagements aside, I'd never found the city to be anything other than a welcome environment for my quieter nature, and began to consider the ways that people like me find a spiritual space and physical place for ourselves in it.

## IN MY OWN COMPANY

It's often assumed that introverts are antisocial and anti-people. Of course we're all different, but that's not true of me and, I'd wager, of very few others who see themselves as being quieter souls. I identify with introverted traits because I like to have time to myself and it is imperative to my sense of well-being. Generally, my best thinking is done alone, too.

Knowing this, I've always made a point of seeking out places of peace in the cityscape, away from all the stimulation. Personally, I find that peace in the botanic gardens or the grand parks of which my home city has so many. In one park in particular, where the horticultural college I studied at for a time was based, I used to abscond to its vast, circular rose garden at lunchtime and sit by myself on the grass between the curved borders. In summertime it was heavenly, busy with vibrant blooms and scented air. I'd feel like I was cocooned in my own patch of paradise, where I could close my eyes for a few minutes and reset.

Not every city is so blessed with green, but spaces that allow 'alone time' don't have to be. It could be a quiet courtyard, a temple or church. City bookstores often have cafés attached to them, where you can grab a cup of tea and escape deep into a book you've just purchased without anyone bothering you.

Solitude isn't always necessary, however. The city is a place where spending time alone is considered valid; apart from anything else, people are often so busy with their own days that nobody is taking any notice of you, or thinking twice about seeing someone enjoying the city this way.

Escapism, in this sense, is available in myriad forms. Public spaces in the metropolis are, more often than not, full of people spending time on their own –

working on laptops, reading or sometimes drawing. It's not unusual to see people wandering art galleries or museums or queuing up for a matinee solo, either.

I once got talking to a young man in London's Royal Festival Hall as I was doing an informal interview of people using the space for a magazine article. He was there to make portraits of people passing through on their way to concerts. He told me it was his favourite place in the city because it allowed him to be alone but also connected, allowing him to draw energy from the buzz without having to chat to anyone, or explain himself (except, that day, to me!). The French novelist Émile Zola would have described him as one of the 'great silent crowds watching the street live' – someone simply happily and quietly existing among the throng of the many.

# City
# Hideaways

---

Togetherness is wonderful for the soul but it remains crucial that we have times of physical solitude, times that relieve us from the sharp elbows of crowds. Solitude is a little gift we can give ourselves. It offers us a chance to switch off from the constant distractions that follow us around most days and replenish our minds; it gives us space to connect with that inner voice and think deeper thoughts than our to-do lists allow.

The fact that a city might not offer the typical hideaways that help revive the spirit – a secluded shore or woodland, or proximity to them – does not mean we cannot discover spaces in it that allow us to be alone. It seems inconceivable in the densely populated city that there could ever be an occasion when we would barely brush by another soul. And so often, therefore, instead of making time in our lives to actively seek out hiding places, we are passive in allowing our 'alone time' to always happen in the close company of others.

As useful as they are for many tasks, mobile phones have made us less inclined to be creative users of time. This thought occurs every time I observe a train pull away from a station and witness carriages packed with commuters scrolling screens, isolating themselves into a digital cocoon, a virtual garden shed, of alone time.

But all our phones do, in this respect, is provide an illusion of separation. Staring at screens may seal us from the pack and allow us to disappear down the rabbit warren of the Internet, but all the while our minds are on duty – absorbing information, communicating, organizing calendars. And when a new message strikes, and we're alerted to it by that excitable ping, we become prisoner of the pressure of having to respond, promptly, constructively, with good humour – it's a very modern-day pressure that saps so much mental energy and impacts our powers of concentration.

## AN ESCAPIST PURSUIT

At times when you don't have a choice, such as during the commute to work, perhaps you can dedicate a few journeys in the week to losing yourself in a novel instead of your emails. Books, in my view, are a much more rewarding escapist experience than reading phones because they provide a pause in the constant stream of communication we too often allow ourselves to indulge in. But they also transport us to an entirely new world, one that we get to roam about alone and at our own pace.

Reading our physical environment like we would a book is another escapist pursuit, as we make time to look with that same sense of wonder. Try setting aside a day or a few hours, once a month, where you challenge yourself to break from the pack and immerse yourself in an urban oasis, the way you might a great story.

Choose anywhere that allows the mind to closely observe your physical space in peace, to notice how the shape, sound, texture and colour of it seems alive and present. Early mornings at the weekend are ideal for reading the city this way, as avoiding crowds can sometimes be about timing rather than place.

Forgo the lie-in and arrive at the museum on the hour that it opens, when the rest of the city is asleep, before the snaking queues have a chance to form, so you may ponder the artefacts with the corridors all to yourself. Then, head to your favourite café to breakfast on the freshest pastries of the day, delight in the pleasure of unhurried eating – notice how much better it tastes when you don't have anywhere else to be, or have anyone hovering over you to take your table when you leave.

## A BANQUET FOR THE SENSES

A fun way to keep focus on the world around you is to imagine yourself to be a writer sitting down to describe the scene – ask yourself which details you would use to conjure that scene to life, what words would best describe the atmosphere. Any natural spaces you have available provide so much inspiration in this sense. You might take a languid stroll across the bridge that spans the river as the sun rises, and watch the barges chug past or the wrinkles on the water's surface as they morph.

If your city has them, the gardens of palaces or aristocratic homes, botanic gardens or even parks open to visitors at an early hour can be as tranquil as any hilltop as you stroll through their geometric pathways, manicured shrubberies and ornate flowerbeds in the creamy morning light.

Even in winter, when the tourists have migrated, these spaces are especially meditative. With no one else to navigate around, you're free to let the senses unfurl, to revel in the balletic twirl of the tree's last leaf of the year pirouetting to the ground, the twinkles in the fur of frost that coats each twig, grass blade, crumb of soil. It is a banquet for the senses, spread out only for you – well, you and the birds already up hunting for worms.

# Take a
# Night Walk

The light that falls on the city is a unique version of the night. It isn't a black cloak that wraps around us, and it has no inky depth. The hazy orange halo that typically domes a city skyline means it isn't a place for deep sleeping; nor is it a place for gazing at stars. Rather, the night of the city is a raucous cabaret, a busy theatre of neon advertising boards, streets studded with car lights, office blocks glowing with the lights that keep after-hours devotees company. A silent night it is not, but it is a beauty that we have conjured.

Imagine how the effervescence of the city at night looks to the eyes that view it from afar. On one brief, hectic work trip to San Francisco, during which I'd had no time to sightsee, I'd been tipped off that the best way to spend the hours I had left before my plane home was to take a cab to the other side of the Golden Gate Bridge after dark and look at the city from the viewing point there.

Staring at the luminous metropolis across the water, I could trace where I had come from by the two tracks of lights lining either side of the bridge. It appeared as if they were running back towards the city, like coins marking the route to a giant treasure trove. Though I had no time to enjoy all that I could imagine happening back there, it was still energizing to think of it; the friends who would be enjoying burrito nightcaps after the dance floors close; the literature enthusiasts browsing bookstore shelves for Beat poetry; the cinemas that would be showing movies at midnight, the sound of laughter rising from the comedy clubs into the sky.

I decided that to see the city like this, a dazzling beacon in the abyss, must be a very small something of what it is to see the Earth from space; where all the chaos is dimmed down, appears serene and silent, in an endless universe of who knows what else.

## CREATE A CONTRAST

Back in the midst of the city, we experience a night that could not be further from the one our ancestors enjoyed, with nothing more than a small fire and the stars for illumination once the sun set. These 24/7 lifestyles we've developed have, arguably, helped us to achieve more in a day, but they certainly come at a price. Experiencing the dark is good for us; it is natural to our biology, crucial for restorative sleep and keeps our immune system functioning. Living in a place that barely sleeps can, therefore, be a draining aspect of urban living.

Ensuring that we have as much time as possible in the quiet and dark is a mindful exercise we can practise at home, by making these environments less stimulating than the streets outside. Keeping evenings as calm and low-lit as possible is within our control, and we can switch off phones, TVs, computers and lamps, all of which can be disruptive to the body's biology when we sleep.

We can then better appreciate the city at night when we are out there, experience it in a positive way as opposed to a mental drain. Our mind is less charged, more open to seeing the city at night as beautiful in its own way. Open to observe more, we see the changing colours of the darkening sky and take in the aromas of exotic foods drifting out from restaurant kitchens. My most vivid memories of the cities I've visited are their nightscapes. Somehow, it seems that this is the time when their personalities truly shine, when what is distinct about them becomes prominent.

## MERE FLICKERS

Taking a night walk with the distinct purpose of aimlessness reveals features of the city's personality special to that time of day. As we walk, we can glimpse the moon above us. Turning our eyes upwards to see this postmark of another dimension, one beyond the city limits, is a reminder of our place in the solar system. Far from making us feel insignificant as we consider how brief our lives are compared with the eternal space the moon inhabits, glancing at the moon allows us to reflect on the precious nature of the now. Reminding ourselves, every once in a while, that we are mere flickers in the life of a planet over four billion years old can be an uplifting, life-affirming meditation – one that motivates us to feel thankful that we were ever present to experience it at all.

# The Colour
## of Winter

My bones would tell me that winter
was upon me, if I did not have eyes to
see it for myself. At these times, when
those night-afternoons lie heavy on
a shallow day of weakened sun, my
skeleton aches deeply. It isn't just the
cold weather. I need strategies to
bear the decay of the organic in the
urban, as once rampant vegetation
withers from railway sidings,

summer balcony displays and gardens; as once blowsy
flower borders shrivel into mounds of lank, dead plants,
and picnic-perfect park grass lies depressed in the mud.

In wintertime, there's a sense that the entire city is wallowing in a muddy puddle. In its state of gloomy quietude, hectic jobs and short days can make it hard to engage with what is vibrant about city life. And spending much of the brief day cooped up indoors can be a struggle – it is tough to retain a sense of connection to the city beyond windows furred with frost.

## COLOUR THERAPY

Colour is my remedy, so on gloomy Sundays I will often make a trip to art galleries in search of a nurturing pick-me-up. Psychologists and art therapists are well aware of how colour can influence our mental or physical state – red can send adrenaline rushing to the bloodstream, blue, green and purple can induce feelings of calm, and the colour orange can bring a sense of warmth.

Galleries are rich resources of colour therapy and common to most cities. Not only is a visit to an art gallery cheaper than a sunny getaway, but galleries are forever changing, with a regular turnover of artists and paintings, so there is always something fresh to look at.

Once ensconced inside, away from the drudgery of the weather, you can find yourself in the midst of a more exhilarating landscape, one of peaceful white walls juxtaposed with the loud vibrant paint on canvas. To keep your mind focused, you could study the rooms for one or two colours in particular. I, for one, am always drawn to the liberal blocks of cheery and optimistic yellows found in abstract paintings.

Resting the gaze for a while on one piece in particular, even just one colour in an entire composition, I begin to imagine the colour beaming straight into my brain. It's in city galleries, either at home or when travelling, that I've experienced colour at its most intense, its most real, its most alive; metre upon metre of Jackson Pollock's carefully wrought, multi-layered and densely textured colours, splashes and lines in MOMA; Claude Monet's iridescent lilies in the Musée de l'Orangerie in Paris.

Paintings are portals that transport us to a brighter, lighter world than the one of our daily experience; they enable us to connect with emotions other than our own. As the painter Wassily Kandinsky believed, colour – like musical sounds – is a gateway to the soul. As far as spiritual renewal goes, the galleries of our cities can be as uplifting as the first spring buds.

On one dreary November afternoon several years ago, I visited an exhibition of Turner's seascapes in London's National Maritime Museum. There were over one hundred pieces featuring the elemental power of the sea, including oils, watercolours and sketches of sunsets, storms, swells and shipwrecks in roiling waters – created from a palette of cobalt blue, white, deep navy and emerald green. It is alleged that Turner lashed himself to the mast of a ship to better capture its force; how lucky, I thought, to be able to exist so close to such legendary mastery, only a few miles from my front door. I could almost feel the water's spray brushing against my face – as if I were perched on the edge of a remote coastline.

## EMBRACE STREET ART

You needn't know anything about art to appreciate the simple power of colour, but if galleries really aren't for you, then consider where else you could meditate upon it. Churches or cathedrals are often home to vast installations of stained glass in a rainbow of colour. And in some cities, you may even find public works such as murals or street art displayed in subways, or on walls or bridges. Cities such as Philadelphia, Melbourne, London, Washington and New York have embraced stylistic graffiti and stencil art in the public domain, with festivals dedicated to the art form or allowing buildings to be used as giant concrete canvases. Such urban art is – perhaps – an acquired taste, but the best works can evoke the vigour and creativity of the street, and reconnect us to a very distinct urban energy from which those winter months can so easily alienate us.

# Let the Rain
# Soothe You

There is no such thing as the wrong weather, asserts the rambler, only the wrong clothing. It's not so easy for the city dweller to embrace the same sanguinity. Rain, or worse, drowns weekend fun – sports games, parks and playgrounds. It is the promise of a miserable commute ahead as you crowd under the bus shelter with everyone else, shoes, socks, tights and toes thoroughly soaked already.

When we see rain pounding the pavements, it doesn't charm us the way it would charm the rambler, dressed head to toe in waterproofs, watching it drop in delicate beads on a leaf, or falling, way out at sea, from a cloud gliding across the horizon.

Yet rain in the city is the same substance as it is in any landscape. So even as we observe rain pelting buildings and spattering windscreens, we can reflect that this is the weather that has brought happiness at other moments – perhaps hearing it drum on windows while tucked up by the fireside, or sensing the relief of the earth as the rain cracks the thick crust of a hot sky.

We may also reflect that the arrival of rain in the city is a pit stop on a long journey from many places – one of constant change that continues in our urban environments, first tumbling from the sky as droplets, then renewing as a stream in the gutters or forming a patina on roofs. Before long, it is again vanished, having found its way back to the atmosphere, where it will morph again from liquid to vapour to crystals of ice.

## IN CONTEMPLATION OF WATER

Rain has the same contemplative properties as water, a feature I've noticed lately appearing with greater frequency – and prominence – in public spaces across many cities. These days, it's not uncommon to see water being incorporated in ever more inventive ways: playful water jets shooting from the paving, dwelling spaces designed around extensive mirror pools or even slim streams running through channels created in paving. Many of these are adding to well-established fountains or other aquatic installations that have belonged to the cityscape for centuries.

Observing water in motion makes me mindful of what is required in the present moment. When it is time to do so, water rolls and runs; when stillness is called for, it rests. It also reminds me that letting go of emotional and physical baggage helps to keep the spirit light, because water does not cling – its surface reflects the moment for as long as it endures. A river will tolerate all that travels with it, both beautiful and ugly – shoals of fish, tin cans, pebbles and weeds – but is attached to none.

Water-centred designs well understand that you don't need a sea view to feel connected to the potent therapeutic potential of water. Water is part of us, an essential and major component of our physiology. I believe this is why its presence and sound has a calming and uplifting effect on us, in whatever form it appears. After all, the element is life-giving and life-sustaining – qualities possessed by rain in equal measure. So as it is soaking me to the bone, I try to remember how vital it is. I try to accept its inconvenience as a reminder of our lack of control over many things, and remember it is sometimes better to accept than to fight an unwelcome downpour. In simply knowing that there is little I can do to avoid getting wet, I may even find I enjoy the sensation of water tickling my skin.

## A PICTURE OF PURE EASE

I was reminded of this during a visit to Berlin's Brandenburg Gate – a former symbol of the political division that separated East from West during the Cold War but which became an emblem of unity on Germany's reunification. Seated cross-legged on the drenched ground close to the gateway was a circle of twenty or so people, holding umbrellas to shelter from the beating raindrops.

They were meditating; they did not move for all the time I observed them. For what cause they were there I didn't fathom, but their stillness was undeterred by the chaotic weather and the tourists that snapped photos of them. The group appeared completely relaxed in the presence of that dreary slug-grey scene that would have sent most dashing for cover.

Instead, it was a picture of pure ease. Psychologists encourage us to tolerate uncertainty in life with unconditional acceptance. Our well-being, they believe, depends upon it and is further served by being able to see ourselves as a part of an interconnected whole. It seemed to me that the meditation group had got this idea. We can't change the weather but, wearing the right clothing or not, it is healthy to embrace that which comes our way.

# Create an
# Island of Wild

Thriving urban gardens are rebellious little things. Whenever I see a window box stuffed with herbs, or a teeny backyard hosting a jungle of luscious plants, leaves as large as frying pans, I can't help but think that behind the creation of each there's someone determined to bring beauty to a space, no matter how small.

What makes them equally cheering sights is that they have often been planted to delight not just the gardener themselves, but their neighbourhoods and communities too. I've met and written about many city gardeners, from Tokyo to Los Angeles, and it seems to me that socially focused motivations often drive the desire to plug a few plants into a scrap of compost.

These ambitions can be as simple as the hope that a passer-by, seeing an abundance of flowers, will be uplifted by it, feel better about the streets in which they live. But they can also be more public, political and larger in scale. This is the case in one green movement in San Francisco, where residents have planted miniature parks in the pavements outside their houses, complete with seating and dwelling spaces, to allow and encourage those passing to hang out and enjoy the flowers.

These parks, known as parklets, some only the size of a handful of paving slabs are especially designed for people who might otherwise rarely glimpse the natural world. Plants are positioned low enough to the ground so their scented, gleeful blooms meet the eyes of small children in their pushchairs, or in places accessible to those with mobility issues who cannot easily travel to city parks.

Aside from their aesthetic credentials, parklets are also clever acts of protest – an attempt to reclaim the streets that are far too often designed for cars, and all too often characterized by concrete. How brilliant

to think that even the smallest island of wild can
be a way of speaking to the city.

## VERDANT PATCHES

A scatter of pots or a couple of hanging baskets can
change our experience of the city, from one of tyres
and bricks to one of scent, colour and texture. They also
make a statement about how you want the city to be.
Little gardens say to me that the person or community
who made them wish to live in a city that has clean air
and supports pollinators and sustainable ecosystems.

Even the tiniest verdant patches create a purifying
tonic for the surrounding environment; they purify
the air as plants remove carbon dioxide and pump out
oxygen, and provide scraps of soil that absorb rainfall
run-off from impervious roofs and streets. They are
also rich seams of nectar and pollen.

Bees, birds, beetles, bats, butterflies and moths are
suffering dangerous declines all over the globe due to
feeding and·nesting habitat loss, misuse of chemicals and

changes in climate patterns – making islands of flowers, in private or public spaces, ever more vital. Raising these gardens in a limited space has many rewards for the generous grower. When pollinators fertilize your plants, they turn your garden from a collection of buds to a flourishing success – kick-starting reproduction, setting seed for the next season and even ensuring delicious food crops for your dinner plate.

## THE ECOLOGICAL HIGHWAY

However, it is when one island garden takes root near another that things get exciting. Your garden is then part of a network of other gardens, containing diverse flowering plant species that can support an even wider range of pollinators. So not only do they allure wildlife to your outdoor space, they also connect you with other gardens in the city.

How cool it is to be able to imagine your island of wild as part of one ecological highway, working in unison with all the other nearby window boxes, pots, gardens and parks. If your garden is close to an allotment or food-growing project, or even a couple of apple trees, it is helping pollinate fruit and vegetables growing in these spaces because bees, for instance, will transport pollen grains as they move from one flower to another.

It's a neighbourly act, the perfect altruistic gesture. But it is also a meditation on how interconnected we are. Our pollinators need us but they are also one of our most precious resources, indispensable to almost all the flowering plants on Earth for reproduction. Without them, countless fruits, vegetables and nuts, as well as oils, fibres and raw materials, simply wouldn't exist. So while our city gardens may be small, they keep us in touch with these momentous ideas.

# Trust
## the City

I once visited a pop-up garden created by the residents of a London street. Named the Edible Bus Stop, the little farm had, as the name suggests, been planted around a bus stop to transform a bland stretch of concrete into a verdant patch.

Potatoes, gooseberries and herbs, among an assortment of other goodies, were grown for anyone passing to harvest. The Edible Bus Stop brought lush softness to the hard lines of a boisterous urban road – but just as striking was its ethos.

The garden had no padlocked gates or fences to protect crops from uncivil acts. I asked the volunteers about this relaxed approach during my interview. 'We have tried to create the sense that the garden is for everyone,' they explained.

The gardeners were right to have placed trust in their neighbours: the Edible Bus Stop never once suffered an act of vandalism. And their request to donate a packet of seeds or lend a hand if you picked produce was mostly honoured.

This wasn't the first time I'd come across a community project that had been respected by the hundreds of people who came into daily contact with it. Another was a wildflower meadow next to a football field. Nearby residents had objected to plans for the meadow on the grounds that the kids who played ball games on the pitches alongside would be careless towards the planting. But during a talk on urban nature a year after the seeds were sown, the volunteer who'd overseen the project presented a report that showed the meadow had not been trampled over at all, and was in fact flourishing in its first summer.

## LOOK FOR THE GOODNESS

Anecdotes like these challenge the default view that it is best to distrust humanity – and how ironic that they both hail from a city that has a reputation for being a less safe place to live than a tight-knit village where everyone knows your name.

My mother, who lives rurally, subscribes to this view, believing cities to be dangerous and packed with 'weirdoes'. The city she knows, the one my partner and I raise our children in, is the city she sees on the 24-hour news, the one that only reports the bad stuff. 'You just don't know what kind of person you'll be sitting next to,' she says of public transport.

My feeling, however, is that living alongside so many people, as we urbanites do, has the potential to nurture an instinct to believe in others. The more people we meet and the greater amount of humanity we are exposed to, the more evidence we see that most humans are essentially kind beings. We all have urban horror stories to share, and in certain circumstances our wits must be sharp. But the more we interact, the more opportunity we have to neutralize bad experiences and rebuild our faith.

## WITHOUT PREJUDICE

Over the time I recently spent away from the city, living instead in a very small village, I met some wonderful, beautiful people, but also witnessed bizarre acts of greed and possessiveness and encountered an ingrained suspicion of 'outsiders', which included anyone who wasn't born in the area. This experience, for me, challenged the idea that community spirit thrives more freely in small communities compared with more populous places.

Cities are just as adept at fostering trust and a sense of community as anywhere because they are so open and diverse. Trust grows out of people interacting with one another and the more of those interactions we have with others, the more at ease with humanity we can be – wherever it is we find ourselves living.

Living in a state of distrust is the easiest thing to do. But meditating on the countless instances of trust we encounter in the metropolis nourishes peace within and goodwill towards others. When we encounter rubbish and upsetting behaviour, it is tempting to blame it on the intrinsic character of the city, to tell ourselves it encourages people to be self-centred and rude. But next time that does happen, trying to refrain from watering that seed of negativity and thus allowing it to blossom, might make us feel better.

Instead, study what happens around you without prejudice. Tot up the interactions over the rest of the day. Examine how those you walked, travelled, shopped alongside treated you – you may be pleasantly surprised to find many more instances of goodwill. As the gardeners who had faith in their neighbours discovered, we can't experience community spirit until we trust that it is there.

# Build a
## Communal City

Sharing is a way of life in cities. When so many millions cohabit upon relatively small patches of land, it's inevitable.

Swimming pools, libraries and galleries are busier than we'd find in the countryside, and with gardens out of the question for most urbanites living in apartments, public parks are our only access to organic wonders. This is communal living in its broadest sense. Sometimes having to jostle with others wherever we go is claustrophobic. But in so many pockets of the city there are opportunities to make the most of that closeness, and to be part of a community group that connects us with one of the most spiritually uplifting forms of mindfulness available.

Enriching urban communities come in many forms; the fabulous thing about cities is that whatever issue you hold dear, you'll find a like-minded group you can join. One form of collective mindfulness that's flourishing is in response to environmental problems, as city dwellers find ways to lower resource impact through car-sharing schemes and solar energy cooperatives, while concerns over food security have also seen a coming together of communities in many cities. Created by people from across the socio-economic and demographic spectrum, action groups are making food accessible, nutritious and sustainable for neighbourhoods on full-scale city farms, roadside allotments and even waste ground.

## A REWARDING EXISTENCE

It's a refreshing alternative to our tendency to focus inwards as we strive to make ends meet and provide a decent lifestyle for our families, or ourselves. These pressures can be isolating, making life seem a lonely struggle. But in communal actions – whether sharing goods, knowledge, skills or space – we find a more social and rewarding way to exist.

Hard outcomes aside, in the act of creating nutritionally rich food or bringing solar panels to housing estates, you can discover a sense of belonging and common purpose as you make change happen alongside neighbours you might otherwise ignore. Tilling the soil as you chat to a new friend two doors away, or helping to raise funds to rescue a local green space, gives us a chance to be with others who care about making our cities more pleasant. It also exposes us to a side of humanity easy to forget when our only interaction with the world is through the prism of news bulletins. Knowing that such caring, positive people live on your doorstep is a refreshing mental tonic.

I once interviewed a lady in Harlem who, living alone, found weekends a depressing endeavour, as friends busied themselves with their partners and kids. Hitting the shops had been her way of getting out of the house and giving her Saturdays a structure, until she was invited to join a community garden that had taken root, thanks to the enthusiasm of residents, on an abandoned, weedy parking lot nearby. Having no garden of her own, she relished the opportunity to handle seeds and soil. But much more than this, she told me, was that being part of the garden had given her spiritual fulfilment; in helping to supply fresh food to poor families, she found a sense of achievement unique to the act of serving others.

## COMMUNAL MINDFULNESS

Mindful communities don't have to be the preserve of neighbourhoods. Demanding jobs mean that time spent at home can be limited, making it hard to join in local action groups. However, workplace culture is becoming more attuned to the mental and physical benefits of communal activities, as businesses realize they boost employees' well-being, decrease sick days and work wonders for staff retention.

Rooftop gardens are an urban phenomenon that has introduced mindfulness to the 9–5, as employees take part in lunchtime gardening clubs or use these beautified spaces for a screen break, while some companies, in a bid to engage in true social initiatives as opposed to faceless monetary donations, have launched their own community groups.

A friend of mine joined one that brought beehives to a forbidding bit of concrete on her workplace roof. It blossomed into a social enterprise for the area, using bees as a way to work with local teenagers, who were enlisted to help run it, building skills and confidence in themselves in the process.

Such communal mindfulness might not be a feature of your own workplace, but there are enough examples of it about to support an idea you might wish to introduce, convincing any unenlightened boss of the benefits. As he or she should know, the age-old notion of community spirit is alive, kicking and possible anywhere.

# Be with
# Others

It is easy to perceive mindfulness as a pot of gold at the end of a rainbow – to conceptualize its nature as a state of being that exists once we make our escape from the city. A windblown heathland, a rolling blue sea, a stroll along a beachscape devoid of human attention – these are typical forums in which we aim to relax and finally 'find' our deeper selves. It can often feel as though letting go of our anxieties is only possible like this.

I'm not undermining the healing qualities that landscape effects on a stressed-out urban brain. We now know so much, thankfully, of our need for contact with roots and shoots, for fresh air. Humans – in one form or another – roamed the Earth for millions of years, a long, long time before the creation of concrete, so it is of course crucial, and for all of us, to make contact with spaces (both tiny and vast) away from skyscrapers and the suburbs. But mastering mindfulness cannot be achieved by overlooking the unrivalled power that connecting with humanity can wield.

A city's 'hustle and bustle' is often used as a euphemism for all that is wrong with our life set-up. Seeing our cheek-by-jowl proximity to humanity in this way can be a negative take on our urban environment that stands in the way of an appreciation of it. And not many of us possess the ability to take ourselves off to the wild often enough for it to be a reliable mindful tonic. What is more, humanity is our reality.

## A PART OF PURE HUMANITY

The seeds of a balanced, peaceful mental state do not exist in the soil. They rest dormant in our minds, and at all times. And this means that being part of a local choir or visiting the exhibition of a magical painter has the ability to germinate the seeds of mindfulness just the same as a walk in woodland. These activities all have the same value; it is only our perception of them that differs.

One Christmas recently, our first living back in London after our stint in the wilds of West Cornwall, we headed to a carol concert at the Royal Albert Hall. It was the first time since our return that we'd taken the opportunity to engage in a cultural event. Late arriving, some ten minutes after the start, the concert was already in full swing as we entered the hall to take our seats. The auditorium was packed with people – dressed in festive jumpers, some had wrapped themselves in Christmas lights, and they were merrily belting out the lines of 'Jingle Bells'.

The noise was consuming, joyous. It was overwhelming to hear these thousands of voices in unison, working together to create this mountain of sound. In our rural life, the sounds of the landscape – the ocean, birds cawing, the eerie howl of winds – had the ability to make me feel isolated and alien to my environment. Here, I felt part of what this was – pure humanity.

## A NEED FOR TOGETHERNESS

Years ago, I visited a community pottery to write a story on its (eventually successful) struggle to fight closure. The pottery offered free classes for children from low income families, carers, the homeless and the elderly. The council that owned the land was proposing to demolish the building and replace it with expensive apartments. Chatting to the students there during my visit, I realized what a luxury the desire for isolation is.

Muriel, 83, who lived alone, told me she came to class every Wednesday – the only activity she did all week. Kevin, a young man who'd been homeless when he began coming to class, had gained enough skills from his time in the pottery to secure a job at a local supermarket. And Mary, another elderly student, summarized the value of all of this best, 'I missed class last week and I felt terrible. It is the only place some people here can come to; they don't see anybody else otherwise. If we don't keep hold of spaces where we share experiences, people here will lose confidence.'

Leo Hollis, in his book *Cities are Good for You*, says, 'We have a biological need to be together … For Jean-Paul Sartre, hell was other people, but the chain-smoking existentialist was wrong.' When a random gathering of people turns into a community – be it a carol concert, a food-growing project, a protest march – we discover the power of sharing time. We realize how much pressure we place on ourselves to make moments count, to make sense of our place in the world. But the simple act of 'joining in' alleviates the burden of doing it alone, and is sometimes all that we really need.

# Love the
## Urban Species

Invite a person who has never lived in the city to describe the traits of an urbanite and I'd wager they might list our go-getting ways, our propensity for stress and an obsession with money. They might also say that we all walk too fast and that we're rude and aggressive, especially when it comes to securing the last spot on a crowded train. And they may even venture that we are all crazy for choosing a life that demands us to exist so pressed up against one another.

The English writer William Blake once wrote, 'Where man is not, nature is barren.' How true. Blake scholars and enthusiasts derive much more learned interpretations of these words, but the line, from *The Marriage of Heaven and Hell*, resonates with the way I see the city – because to live in a place where we are isolated from other humans might, you could argue, be considered even crazier.

It is easy to overlook that making a connection to others beyond our own four walls is intrinsic to finding a sense of home, to establishing a sense of who we are and who we are not. There was a time when I didn't see that. Running a diary that had, week after week, always felt overpacked – with dinner dates, with commitments for work I hadn't enough time to meet, appointments north, south, west and east – I came to believe that a life where I answered to as few people as possible was the ideal.

I was wrong about that. In a little café by the sea, at the furthest western tip of the country, where I was searching in vain for peace in the quiet life, I received a wise slice of advice on the recipe for happiness. 'You can never allow yourself to shrivel up,' said the holidaymaker, a grandfather of six to whom I'd got chatting on the table opposite. 'The more you connect with others, the more energy you have for life.'

And there it was, the reason I had found it so hard to feel at ease hundreds of miles from the city I loved, from the people I knew: I was shrivelling up. I'd spent my twenties and most of my thirties in London and all the while I had been there, without being conscious of it, I had learned to thrive on its buzz. I now see that when cities are described as having 'buzz', what this actually alludes to is the dynamic energy that's created when people spend time together, talking, working, inventing and collaborating. A city feels exciting, it *is* exciting, because it is a colossal sum of all the sparks of human interaction.

## THE MOST PEACEFUL MESSAGE

Some of us can, of course, adapt to isolation. Some of us can live in small villages and find community. But in my own case, I discovered that the city was my community and having been so much a part of it, I would never find it easy to nurture peace in my own mind by looking inward – indeed, it is debatable whether anyone truly can.

Cities are communities that draw us outside of ourselves. And so often they can be places that wear their diversity – of race, culture, religion and sexual orientation – not as a threat but as a badge of honour, as unquestionably fundamental to its identity, and that is a very positive environment to belong to. In any community that is open this way – as cities often are – we learn how to overcome our differences. Peace, mindfulness gurus tell us, is not found by focusing on our individual identity, by striving to feed our ego, and it is this that is the source of so much angst, of so much dissatisfaction.

It seems obvious to me that the more people we meet, the more personalities and cultures we experience, the greater chance we have of seeing our own selves in perspective; we also begin to understand the strength of our social species, and the reality of our interdependence. We may find this in any place, but for sure we find such opportunities in the metropolis.

We have an intrinsic need for nature; it can tell us much about a mindful way of life. But we cannot remove human beings from that equation. We *are* nature; we are cells, we are atoms, we are part of the physical phenomena of the Earth. We have seen many awful consequences resulting from our tendency to separate nature from human, country from city, trees from tarmac. And we are approaching a time when it is necessary for the survival of our species to see the lie of these distinctions.

While it is undeniable that there is comfort in the escapism of a cliff path, the echoes of a cave, the tangle of woodland, to me the language of humanity has the potential to convey the most peaceful message of all. And it is walking the chaotic, noisy streets in the cities that we have built – under the vast, unknowable sky and upon landscapes millions of years old – where I hear this message loudest.

We are meant to be together.

# ACKNOWLEDGEMENTS

My sincere thanks go to Monica Perdoni, my
commissioning editor, who invited me to write this
book; to Tom Kitch, Jenny Campbell and Jenni Davis
for their support and guidance, and thoughtful
editorial steer on content; to James Lawrence and
the design team at Leaping Hare Press; and to
Lehel Kovacs for his beautiful artwork.